ideals®
CHRISTMAS

There is something about Christmas,
a certain magic that makes a
string of tinsel turn to purest gold
and brings a star straight from heaven
to rest on the tip of every Christmas tree.
—MARY PANSY RAPP

ideals®
NASHVILLE, TENNESSEE

A Special Time
Judy Schwab

Shopping lists, kitchen smells,
children singing "Jingle Bells,"
colored lights, falling snow,
fireplace with amber glow,
trees adorned, a holly bough,
parties, friends, blessings now.
Memories shared, a quiet tear,
some are gone, still wanted here.
A time of peace and hope renewed,
our fellow man, with love imbued—
a host of things, so many more,
to answer, then, what's Christmas for?

Christmas
Pauline Havard

Christmas! The scent of evergreens;
the tall fir tree, bright with tinsel, balls, and star;
the opening of the gifts, I see it all—
for memory holds my childhood's door ajar!
And so, though time has made a gulf between
each old, enchanted Christmas of the past,
I smell the loved scent of the evergreen
and know the memory will always last—
a healing fragrance in the lonely night,
a glowing flame that keeps the heart alight.

Country Chronicle

Lansing Christman

Come walk with me this sunny Christmas morning to a grove of pines. (My father called them watchtowers for the hawks and crows, turrets for the owls.) It is one of my favorite sanctuaries at any time of year. Its carpet of dried needles is the only luxurious rug I shall ever know, and its aroma exhilarates me. I stand to listen and the pines whisper to me in tender, wistful tones.

Here, last night's snow has blanketed forest and field and capped the reaching boughs of the stately evergreens. No wind stirs as we pass under a silent bower of white. The purity of this outdoor cathedral reflects the holiness of this season. As the artistry of nature unfolds before me, I know I am watching the handiwork of God; and my heart is filled with the splendor of creation.

Pines inspire me. They have felt the lash of winds, the burden of ice, the weight of snow; but they have endured. I gaze with awe into their spires, towering heavenward like the steeple on the old country church of my boyhood.

It is Christmas, when again I become a child of the hills who seeks the wonders of creation and the beauty of nature, who exults in the birth of our Savior. Here, I find joy and solace as I feel Christ's love for mankind and His message of love and everlasting peace.

As I peer into the treetops, I hear once more the psalmist's words: "I will lift up mine eyes unto the hills, from whence cometh my help."

World of Winter Snow

Virginia Blanck Moore

All around the house tonight,
all around the town,
feathery flakes of crystal snow
are drifting gently down.
They dim the shape of
　tree and shrub
and pad the walk with white
and make each streetlamp's
　golden rays

look soft as candlelight.
They settle on the windowsill,
creep upward as we stare
in fascination at this wealth
of whiteness everywhere.
Oh, surely even fairyland
with all its magic glow
could not be lovelier than this
white world of winter snow!

Fresh Snowfall

Kay Hoffman

A fresh snowfall in winter
always brings my heart delight
when I waken in the morning
to a wonderland of white.

No pathway leading here or there
to mark the hurried pace,
just fragile etchings in the snow
that wayward branches trace.

How cozy rests each little home
knee-deep in drifts of snow;

smoke curling up from chimneys
adds to the friendly glow.

Fir trees don a regal look
in lavish ermine wrap;
lampposts, too, wear winter's best—
white muffler and top hat.

Our little town so peaceful is
a wonderland of white,
a picture postcard sent from God
to bring our hearts delight.

Festive, snowy street in Boston, Massachusetts. Image © CO Leong/Shutterstock

Sleigh Bells

Elma Helgason

Our modern ways of travel
are surely swift and grand;
we dash about in comfort
by air or sea or land.

But sleigh bells softly ringing
across the drifted snow
remind me of the journeys
of Christmas long ago.

And oft there comes before me
a picture from the past
where dear ones in a farmhouse
heard sleigh bell sounds at last.

I see the ponies plodding
through miles of drifted snow,
and faces at a window
alight with lamplight glow.

And in the frosty twilight,
the tinkling bells sound sweet,
with sound of sliding runners
and crunch of horses' feet.

Through weeks of isolation
in wintry storm and blast,
the sound of tinkling sleigh bells
meant company at last!

In spite of modern travel,
it sets my heart aglow
to hear the sound of sleigh bells
across the miles of snow.

EVENING SLEIGH RIDE *by Darrell Bush.*
Image © Darrell Bush/MHS Licensing

Christmas at Our House

A. Earl Morris

It's Christmastime at our house,
a time of joy and cheer,
a time for which we watch and wait—
the high point of the year.

The greeting cards the postman brings
pile higher every day,
with love expressed in loveliness,
a truly thoughtful way.

For weeks, it seems, there's been an air
of glad and sweet suspense,
of rustlings here and whispers there,
expectancy intense.

Doors festooned with tinsel bright,
arranged by loving hand,
show Christmastime has come again
to this, our happy band.

Each has a place, each has a part
on this the day of days.
No wonder we, with hearts sincere,
sing songs of joy and praise!

Christmas Cards

Alice Arlene MacCulloch

There's something about a Christmas card,
at this time of year,
which brings a special kind of joy
and fills the heart with cheer.

They speed across the lonely miles,
bright Santas in a sleigh;
Oh, what a lovely, cheery thought
these Christmas cards convey.

They come to wish us joy and peace,
with Wise Men and a star,
like joyous Yuletide messengers
from friends both near and far.

Exquisite scenes so beautiful
show us homes and drifted snow,
of children's happy faces
and stockings in a row.

A group of little carolers
sing out lines from "Silent Night";
"May peace, goodwill and happiness
make your Christmas bright."

Every Christmas card's arrival
fills my day with such delight!
May I tuck such love and friendship
into every one I write.

A Very Non-Dairy Christmas

Anne Kennedy Brady

As Christmas approached last year, my husband and I eagerly anticipated sharing the holiday with our five-month-old son, Milo. We sang Christmas carols while we rocked him to sleep each night. We all got dressed up and took professional photos at a local tree lot. And we couldn't wait to take him on his first plane ride to Seattle for a big family Christmas with the grandparents. But shortly before the trip, we learned that Milo was allergic to dairy. Otherwise perfectly healthy, his tiny tummy simply couldn't yet handle this one food; so the pediatrician recommended cutting it from his diet for a while. Since I was still nursing him at the time, this actually meant cutting it from my diet.

I was, of course, a bit disappointed that I'd have to skip the cheeseburgers for a while and opt for almond milk on my cereal. But then I caught sight of the tinseled garland decking the halls of the doctor's office. "What about baked goods?" I asked. The doctor shook her head. "Chocolates?" Nope. My shoulders drooped. "Christmas is coming up," I tried again. She offered a brave smile, "There are so many vegan recipes these days!" I don't know what I expected her to say, but it wasn't that.

On the way home, I swung through the grocery store. The carols piped in overhead did nothing to cheer my spirits as I glumly tossed a container of dairy-free "cheeze" into my basket. Sure, I could learn to love smoothies and sorbet in place of lattes and ice cream. And it would probably help me shed a few stubborn post-baby pounds. But I dreaded the imposition I would become to those around me. Every year, my mother-in-law, Cordelia, hosts a glorious Christmas dinner for the entire family. Both of my brother-in-law's kids are allergic to gluten, eggs, and nuts; so Cordelia is an expert at allergen-free cooking. She could always count on sprucing things up with butter or whipped cream. Now even that was off the table! I imagined that the only thing left of her Christmas spread would be a fruit salad.

On top of that, my in-laws had already spent weeks buying or borrowing baby equipment—bottles, toys, a baby bathtub, even a travel crib—to accommodate us for just a week. I have always prided myself on being low-maintenance; and especially with all the bustle around Christmas, I hated to add one more inconvenience. "Don't worry," Cordelia assured me over the phone the next day. "We'll figure it out!" I was doubtful.

When we arrived at my in-laws' home the week of Christmas, I prepared to apologize my way through the holiday. *I'm sorry, I can't eat the cookies; I'm sorry, I can't eat the mashed potatoes; I'm so sorry I can't eat the pie.* But I never had the chance. My brother-in-law and his family arrived with a huge plate of cookies, and his wife advised me, "The ones with pink sprinkles are dairy-free!" Cordelia announced that she would make a second batch of mashed potatoes with a vegan "buttery spread" she'd discovered. We even found a pumpkin pie recipe that called for non-dairy milk, and topped it with whipped coconut cream! My sweet, gluten-free nephew gave me a big hug at the end of dinner. "It's OK to have allergies, Aunt Anne. Milo can ask me about it sometime."

As the family chatted over dessert and coffee, I shared a smile with my mother-in-law. From day one she has accepted me with open arms and sought to make me feel at home around her table. This year, she transformed what I saw as a challenge into an opportunity to express her love for me in a new way. She extended grace when I was too embarrassed to ask for it. And she showed me that at Christmastime generosity doesn't always look the way we expect. Sometimes it's a pile of presents under the tree. And sometimes it's simply a gallon of almond milk in the fridge. This Christmas, I'm especially grateful for a family that has always treated me like a daughter . . . and never like an imposition!

Dairy-Free Pumpkin Pie

2 eggs
½ cup brown sugar
1½ teaspoons ground cinnamon
½ teaspoon powdered ginger
¼ teaspoon ground cloves
¼ teaspoon ground nutmeg
¼ teaspoon salt

1 tablespoon cornstarch
¾ cup non-dairy milk
1 15-ounce can puréed pumpkin
1 9-inch unbaked pie shell, thawed
    according to package directions
    Whipped Coconut Cream (recipe follows)

Preheat oven to 450°F. Whip eggs until frothy. Beat in brown sugar until well combined. Add spices and salt and mix well. Whisk cornstarch into non-dairy milk then add to batter along with pumpkin. Beat until well blended and smooth. Pour mixture into pie shell. Cover exposed crust with foil. Bake 10 minutes, then reduce heat to 350°F and bake an additional 30 minutes, or until center does not jiggle. Cool completely; serve, topped with Whipped Coconut Cream. Makes 1 pie.

WHIPPED COCONUT CREAM

1 15-ounce can coconut cream
½ cup confectioners' sugar
½ teaspoon vanilla extract

Chill coconut cream overnight to allow cream to separate. Spoon hardened cream into chilled mixing bowl and discard coconut liquid. Beat on high speed for about one minute, until smooth. Add sugar and vanilla, then beat for another 2 to 3 minutes. Use or refrigerate immediately.

Christmas Is Love and Light

Lucille Crumley

*C*hristmas is many things to many people. To me, Christmas means glowing and beautiful things. It means getting the house ready for love. It is the pine tree selected with care. It is trimming the tree with balls and bells, with silver horns and tinsel, with twinkle lights and a smiling angel on top—all of these, gathered through the years, to recall some special Christmas past.

It means hurrying among crowds of people, from store to store, in search of the right gift for someone you love. It means wrapping, with yards of lovely paper and ribbon, that special gift for a special someone.

It means unwrapping the Christmas feeling that we hold in our hearts—the feeling we promised to use more freely during the past year, but somehow got boxed up with the holiday decorations and stored away.

It is pressing your face close to a shop window filled with toys and remembering that red sled you *so* wanted a long time ago. All the years between then and now rush in with sweet nostalgia.

Christmas is a little girl caressing her new doll. It is a little boy in ecstacy over a new bike. It is your son coming home after time away and finding everything the same with those at home. It is a granddaughter writing "Merry Christmas" in a little girl's wobbly scrawl on your frosted window pane.

Christmas is a table decorated with poinsettias and loaded with good things to eat. It is grandmas and grandpas, aunts and uncles and children and grandchildren, gathered around the table; and one special little boy asking the blessing.

Christmas is the joy from Bethlehem when we sing "Silent Night" and "Joy to the World." It is the warmth and faith we feel when our children sing carols at school or take part in the age-old tableau of the Nativity that lifts us out of the present time and carries us far away to Bethlehem.

Christmas is going outside on a crisp December night and looking upward to the cold, shining stars, and remembering the one great star that still leads our hearts to the birthplace of a Child.

Family Recipes

Rice Pudding

½ cup raisins
1 cup medium-grain white rice
2 cups milk
2 tablespoons heavy cream
1 tablespoon salted butter
   Salt
¾ cup sweetened condensed milk

⅛ teaspoon ground cinnamon
⅛ teaspoon ground nutmeg
1 teaspoon vanilla extract
1 egg, beaten
½ cup Caramel-Pecan Sauce
   (recipe follows), honey or melted
   chocolate, optional

In a small bowl, combine raisins and ½ cup water. Set aside for 1 hour.

In a medium nonstick saucepan, combine rice, 2 cups water, milk, cream, butter, and a pinch of salt. Bring to a gentle boil; cover and reduce heat to low and simmer 20 to 25 minutes, stirring twice. Remove rice from heat; stir in sweetened condensed milk, cinnamon, nutmeg, and vanilla. Return to low heat for 5 minutes. Remove from heat and gradually add beaten egg, stirring constantly. Drain raisins and stir in. Serve immediately in 8 small bowls; drizzle 1 tablespoon Caramel-Pecan Sauce, honey, or melted chocolate over each serving, if desired. Makes 8 servings.

Caramel-Pecan Sauce

½ cup butter
½ cup brown sugar

½ cup light corn syrup
½ cup chopped pecans

In a small saucepan over medium-low heat, combine butter, brown sugar, corn syrup, and pecans. Simmer for 5 to 10 minutes, or until mixture begins to caramelize. Remove from heat and allow to cool slightly. Makes 1 cup sauce.

Parmesan Chicken Meatball Casserole

- 1 pound ziti or other small pasta
- 1 pound ground chicken
- 1 cup panko bread crumbs
- 1 egg
- ½ cup grated Parmesan cheese
- ¼ cup milk
- 1 24-ounce jar marinara sauce
- 3 to 4 cups shredded mozzarella cheese
- 1 teaspoon Italian seasoning

Preheat oven to 450°F. In a large pot, bring water to a boil and add pasta, cooking 1 minute less than directed on package; drain. In a large bowl, mix ground chicken, panko, egg, Parmesan, and milk. Form into 1-inch balls and place on a parchment-lined baking sheet. Bake 10 minutes or until cooked through. Remove from oven; reduce oven temperature to 350°F. In a large bowl, toss pasta and meatballs with sauce. In a 9 x 13-inch casserole dish, spread half of pasta and meatballs. Top with half of mozzarella. Repeat with remainder of pasta, meatballs, and mozzarella. Sprinkle Italian seasoning over top. Bake 15 to 20 minutes or until cheese is melted. Makes 10 to 12 servings.

French Onion Soup

- ½ cup butter
- 4 large (or 6 medium) yellow onions, sliced thinly (about 10 cups)
- 4 cups chicken broth
- 4 cups beef broth
- 2 cloves minced garlic
- ¼ teaspoon Worcestershire sauce
- 6 slices French bread or baguette
- 5 to 7 ounces Gruyere cheese, grated

Preheat oven to 400°F. In a soup pot or Dutch oven, melt butter over medium-low heat. Add onions and cook, covered, for 20 minutes. Transfer to oven. Bake, partially covered, 1 hour, stirring halfway through to prevent burning. Return to stove over medium heat; stir to loosen onions from pan. Add broths, Worcestershire sauce and minced garlic; reduce heat to low. Simmer 30 to 45 minutes. Butter one side of the bread slices and broil over low heat until crispy. Ladle soup into oven-safe bowls or ramekins. Place crispy bread on top of each bowl; sprinkle generously with grated cheese. Broil until cheese is melted and bubbly. Serve immediately. Makes 6 servings.

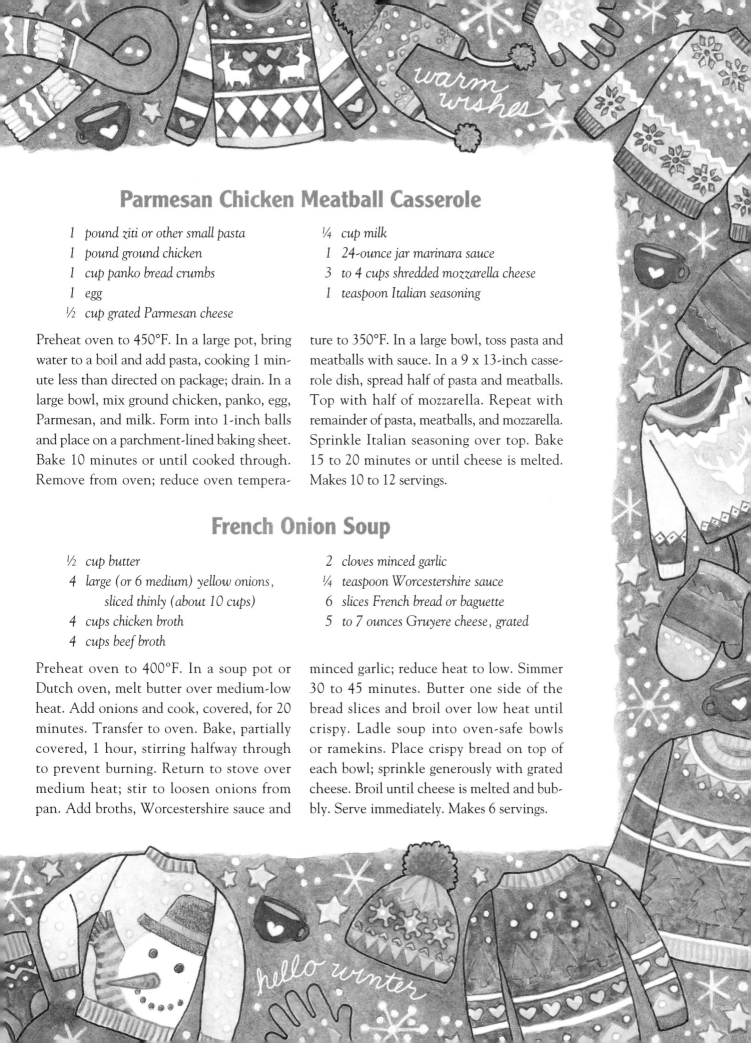

Sparse Decorations

Andrew Luna

I accepted a new job in Georgia during the summer of 1999. However, it took us a little while to find a buyer for our house in Louisville, Kentucky. We finally got a contract during the first part of December, with closing scheduled in January. There was a lot of work to do before we could move. It was not easy packing up a house when I was living almost five hundred miles away and my wife was taking care of our two-year-old twins. During the time I had taken off, we quickly wrapped and packed everything that wasn't essential to our short time remaining in the house. We were faced with the reality that there would be no decorations for Christmas that year. It just wasn't practical. However, I did feel a little sad.

While I tend to be utilitarian, I just had to openly celebrate in a small way. I went to the basement to gaze at all of the boxes we had packed and secured. In the far back was the small Christmas tree I used for my office at work. It would be perfect, because it was easy to set up and take down after the holidays.

I quickly hurried up the stairs, opened the box, and pulled out the tree. Clearly, it was not as grand as our much larger tree. However, it did have a pretty simplicity to it that rekindled a vague recollection of my parents' small tree at the Air Force base where my father was stationed when I was about two. The tree also reminded me that we should be counting all of our bless-ings, large and small. After all, we had finally sold our house and were about to be a family again.

I looked around our den to find a decent place to put the tree. I wanted it on a table where the twins could look at it closely. I chose the table that sat between two recliners. I set the tree on the table and plugged it into the wall. Although sparse, it looked pretty and welcoming.

As the number of days to Christmas short-ened, my wife and I were still busy packing. We did, however, manage to watch some Christmas cartoons and eat some homemade cookies with our twins. During the evening hours, I would turn off all of the lights in the den except for the tree. It filled the room with warmth and happiness, bravely emitting the light of trees much larger and more ornate.

On Christmas Eve, we all gathered around the tree while I read "'Twas the Night Before Christmas." After the story, we put the twins to bed; and my wife and I spent a little quiet time relaxing.

All that day we had been playing Christmas music, watching movies, or playing with the twins—failing to watch any of the local news and weather. I could feel it getting colder when I went outside occasionally, but I had no idea what was in store the next day. Worn out from packing, we went upstairs to bed, leaving the lights on our little tree burning brightly.

When I woke up the next morning, I was amazed to see almost a foot of snow on the lawn.

I was thrilled—the last white Christmas I remembered was when I was four years old. I quickly woke up my wife to wish her a "Merry white Christmas," and I hurried down to the kitchen to make coffee. Our den had a large sliding glass door; and opening the blinds, I could see the snow was packed right up to the edge of the house. Through all of this whitness, our little tree shined bravely and brightly. Then, the reality of everything hit me.

While I enjoyed our little tree, I had missed our larger tree, the mantle decorations, and our Christmas village. Looking outside, however, I realized that God had given us the best decorations. It was a *live* Christmas village, complete with real snow—the kind of natural beauty that could not be imitated by man-made objects. Looking out on the lawn, I noticed the snow covered our green holly trees that were teeming with large, red berries sparkling in the sunlight. As the children came down to open their presents, I marveled at the beauty of it all and was filled with joy and

Image © GAP Photos/Friedrich Strauss

gratitude. That year, God had helped us decorate for Christmas—and used our sparse little tree to make me appreciate the abundance we had.

Happy Eve

Ellie Van Wicklen

Twilight quickly settled,
snowflakes sifted down,
cheery fires crackled
on every hearth in town.

Eager little children
hung their stockings high,

happy men and women
worked fast, as time sped by.

Distant church bells, pealing
glad tidings, oh-so-clear,
brought to all the feeling
of Christmas warmth and cheer.

Then, sweet voices caroled
'neath the window sill
and, in peaceful herald,
a brilliant star stood still.

Earthly peace! Good will to men!
God is with us now, as then.

Christmas Lights

Lucille King

Christmas lights are shining bright
in village streets today;
a star shines bright atop the hill
where children sweetly play.

Christmas lights burn soft and low
on fragrant pine and fir
and dance 'mong snow-flocked
    evergreens
and holly round the door.

Christmas candles, soft and low,
their light on tables shed
and cast small halos on the snow
where stands a manger bed.

Little "lights" are glowing bright
with joy and glad surprise . . .
these are the ones I love
    the best—
the lights in children's eyes.

Home for Christmas

Linda Heuring

Being home for Christmas isn't as much fun as coming home for Christmas. For the first twenty years of my adult life, I traveled over lots of rivers and through dozens of woods to arrive home for the holidays.

Every few years, there was a car a little less likely to break down on the road, a new set of highways from which to view deer at daybreak, or a new speed trap to remind us that the police also worked in the wee hours of the morning.

I've brought a husband, a baby, and at least one dog, all settling into my parents' house for the long winter's nap on Christmas Eve. Santa found us there no matter what state was listed on our driver's licenses.

Our car was laden with baked goods and candy that were more expensive than those from any specialty store because the phone company, not the grocer, reaped the profits from my culinary attempts. The divinity took four long-distance calls (no small expense in those days before cell phones) to my mother, one of which resulted from invariably losing the recipe from one year to the next. I would call to find out whether I was supposed to use evaporated or condensed milk in the bonbons and again to find out the amount of peanut butter in the cookie recipe.

There were also calls to discuss presents when we were sure that certain parties were not listening in on the extension. There were the last-minute messages to let them know what time we were leaving, and there were calls en route if the weather was particularly bad and we knew they'd be worried.

With the help of a book light or the opened glove compartment, cross-stitched napkins were finished in the car on the drive—so were more than one afghan—but for the most part, the drive signaled the beginning of vacation. It was Christmas.

Bursting into my mother's kitchen while carrying a sleeping child or shepherding a barking dog, we'd see every available inch covered with her own holiday baking—the sugar cookies with sour cream icing, the divinity with nuts on top, the rum balls, and the buckeyes. We'd have to move containers of chocolate chip cookies to make room for the sandwiches she'd fix as someone's nonstop talking steamed up the windows.

We'd get our son to bed and keep my parents up way too late listening to music, catching up on the news, shaking presents, and eating.

Time was suspended. Work didn't exist. At home, I'd receive calls from the office, but here it was quiet. All calls were from cousins or brothers. Work was putting the decals on a fighter plane, untangling the controller wire on a video game, or opening my eyes after staying up all night with my brothers and their wives.

For the most part, Christmas was part of a time warp. Going home meant entering a twilight zone of sorts, a place where I could be a kid again, miles from my own house, my job, and my grownup responsibilities. Oh sure, I packed the briefcase of work I couldn't leave behind, but I carried it up to my old room, where it remained until the trip back home.

Living near home for the first time as an adult has put a crimp in my Christmas. Just spending the day with my family isn't quite the same. I miss the anticipation of the trip. My nephews and niece won't have grown much since I saw them last, and when the day's over, I won't be headed up the stairs to my old room to take a nap.

Oh, I guess I could take the long route to my parents' house, but even the long way

is less than a mile. I suppose we could spend the night there, but it doesn't make sense to make all that extra work for my mom when our own beds are just blocks away.

I'm not sorry to be home, just sorry that I can't freeze time and make Christmas last a little longer before I have to go back to my side of town and become an adult again.

Image © Elena Nichizhenova/Shutterstock

Bits & Pieces

I never thought it was
such a bad little tree.
It's not bad at all, really.
Maybe it just needs
a little love.
—*Charles Schulz*

*N*ever worry about the
size of your Christmas tree.
In the eyes of children,
they are all thirty feet tall.
—*Larry Wilde*

O Christmas tree, O Christmas tree,
how lovely are thy branches!
Not only green when summer's here
but in the coldest time of year.
O Christmas tree, O Christmas tree,
how lovely are thy branches!
—*Author Unknown*

TREES &
WREATHS

It won't be long till soon we smell
the balsam and the pine
as through the woods we briskly go
on sleigh rides crisp and fine.
—*Nellie Waites Stokes*

The Christmas tree is a symbol
of love, not money. There's a kind of glory to
them when they're all lit up that exceeds anything all the money in the world could buy.
—*Andy Rooney*

It was the best tree in the world—
the children thought it so.
For such a tree, a hundred times
I'd trample through the snow.
—*Mildred Harper Bell*

The best of all
gifts around any
Christmas tree: the
presence of a happy
family all wrapped up
in each other.
—*Burton Hillis*

The perfect Christmas tree?
All Christmas trees are perfect!
—*Charles N. Barnard*

Christmas Trees

Robert Frost

The city had withdrawn into itself
and left at last the country to the country;
when between whirls of snow not come to lie
and whirls of foliage not yet laid, there drove
a stranger to our yard, who looked the city,
yet did in country fashion in that there
he sat and waited till he drew us out,
a-buttoning coats, to ask him who he was.
He proved to be the city come again
to look for something it had left behind
and could not do without and keep its Christmas.
He asked if I would sell my Christmas trees;
my woods—the young fir balsams like a place
where houses all are churches and have spires.
I hadn't thought of them as Christmas trees.
I doubt if I was tempted for a moment
to sell them off their feet to go in cars
and leave the slope behind the house all bare,
where the sun shines now no warmer than
    the moon.
I'd hate to have them know it if I was.
Yet more I'd hate to hold my trees, except
as others hold theirs or refuse for them,
beyond the time of profitable growth—
the trial by market everything must come to.
I dallied so much with the thought of selling.
Then whether from mistaken courtesy
and fear of seeming short of speech, or whether
from hope of hearing good of what was mine,
I said, "There aren't enough to be worthwhile."
"I could soon tell how many they would cut,
you let me look them over."

    "You could look.
But don't expect I'm going to let you have them."
Pasture they spring in, some in clumps too close
that lop each other of boughs, but not a few
quite solitary and having equal boughs
all round and round. The latter he nodded "Yes" to,
or paused to say beneath some lovelier one,
with a buyer's moderation, "That would do."
I thought so too, but wasn't there to say so.
We climbed the pasture on the south, crossed over,
and came down on the north.

He said, "A thousand."

"A thousand Christmas trees!—at what apiece?"

He felt some need of softening that to me:
"A thousand trees would come to thirty dollars."
Then I was certain I had never meant
to let him have them. Never show surprise!
But thirty dollars seemed so small beside
the extent of pasture I should strip, three cents
(for that was all they figured out apiece)—
three cents so small beside the dollar friends
I should be writing to within the hour
would pay in cities for good trees like those,
regular vestry-trees whole Sunday Schools
could hang enough on to pick off enough.

A thousand Christmas trees I didn't know I had!
Worth three cents more to give away than sell,
as may be shown by a simple calculation.
Too bad I couldn't lay one in a letter.
I can't help wishing I could send you one,
in wishing you herewith a Merry Christmas.

Children's Faces

Georgia B. Adams

You can capture all the wonder
of this season if you try;
it is mirrored in the faces
of the children passing by.

See their toothless smiles and hear them
as they shout their shouts of glee;
watch their eyes grow wide and open
when they see the Christmas tree.

When you speak to them of Santa,
they behave like angels sweet.
(And sometimes I think a halo
would just make this scene complete!)

When they open up their presents,
mirrored in each face you'll see
first surprise, then satisfaction
for the gift is sure to please.

You can capture all the wonder
of this season if you try;
it is mirrored in the faces
of the children passing by.

City Christmas Magic

Eileen Spinelli

There is magic in the
    moonlit snow,
in city sleigh bells ringing.
There is magic in the
    courtyard tree
and the red-cheeked
    schoolboys singing.

There is magic in the
    twinkling shops,
in the warm and
    glowing chapels.

There is magic in the
    vendors' carts:
chestnuts, pears
    and apples.

There is magic in the
    hands that crafted
wooden stall and manger.
But most magical of all
    to me
is the kindness
of a stranger.

Christmas Windows

Nadine Brothers Lybarger

Dressed-up Christmas windows sparkle in the night,
arrayed in Christmas splendor, colorful and bright,
with glowing lights and tinsel and presents on a tree—
oh, what a joy is Christmas when hearts go on a spree!

Merchants' windows beckon: *The time grows near,* they say,
when Santa will be coming round—prepare for Christmas Day!
Come see what we've to offer to bring some loved one joy;
you're sure to find that treasured gift, that extra-special toy.

With small red noses pressing up against the window pane,
children stand and, watching them, I am a child again,
remembering that once I too was caught up in its spell
and dreamed of owning everything the merchants had to sell.

Though many things have changed a bit in grownup worlds today,
the same enchantment still is found in every bright display
of heaped-up Christmas treasures these Christmas windows hold,
where children stand with noses pressed, oblivious to cold.

Through My Window

The Friendly Beasts

Pamela Kennedy

In our family, we have a way of doing Christmas. We fill stockings on Christmas Eve and open them on Christmas morning, after coffee but before our traditional breakfast of Julekake. Then we open our tree gifts. We take turns, and everyone has time to relish both giving and receiving. It's how we have done things ever since we were married, almost fifty years ago. When grandchildren arrived, we adapted to naptimes and short attention spans; but the basics of Christmas morning remained the same. Until last Christmas.

Last fall, our forty-one-year-old son, Josh, asked if he could invite his girlfriend, Mel, to join us for Christmas. This was a big deal. Josh hadn't had a girlfriend since college, and inviting someone new into the Christmas fold is no small matter. But we had all met this woman and she was amazing—smart, beautiful, full of joy, and, best of all, she made our son happy. Of course she could join us!

Just after Thanksgiving, Josh mentioned that Mel had some special gifts in mind for each of us, but she wondered if she could present them to us on Christmas Eve. That way, she'd told Josh, we could all enjoy them on Christmas morning. Well, we didn't usually exchange gifts on Christmas Eve, but this was special. Okay. That would be great!

My husband and I shared the news with our other kids and their families—after all, it was a break with our tradition. Younger brother, Doug, and his family were all in. "Whatever makes Josh happy! What do you think the gifts are? Christmas socks?" Sister, Anne, and her family thought it sounded like fun. "Maybe it's Christmas mugs for our morning coffee!" We were all on board. Bring on the Christmas cheer!

Now at this point, I should mention that we're a pretty reserved bunch. With the exception of dancing to a Beatles song at our daughter's wedding, my husband and I don't do "wild and crazy." And even then, we were wearing formal attire. My husband's idea of dressing up for a Halloween party is donning a hat with his regular duds and going as a hat rack. Most of us are introverts. And Josh, in particular, has always refused to do anything to attract attention.

So here we were, gathered around a roaring fire on Christmas Eve, when Josh's sweet Mel announced it was time for her to give us our gifts. The two of them handed out beautiful, large gift bags, bursting with silver tissue paper. "Go ahead," she said. "Everyone open them at once!"

Tissue flew in all directions. Then we all drew a collective gasp as we revealed Mel's gifts: soft, fleecy animal onesies. "Look, Grammy! I'm a cheetah!" four-year-old Henry shouted. His baby sister, Evelyn, waved her kitten suit around and their parents stared in awe at their leopard and panther outfits. "Wow!" chimed in Anne as she and her husband, Kevin, extracted matching giraffe onesies for themselves and their six-month-old son, Milo. Speechless, my husband pulled a brown reindeer suit from his bag, while I held up a snowy white unicorn outfit, complete with a rainbow tail and golden horn! Josh and Mel looked ecstatic. "So everyone will wear their animal jammies tomorrow morning! It will be great!" they announced.

Later, as we put away the dinner dishes and swept up, I asked my husband, "So, how do you feel about wearing a six-foot Rudolph onesie tomorrow?" There was a moment of silence. "Well," he replied, "I've never seen Josh so happy, and I'm not about to rain on that parade!" I smiled and nodded in agreement.

In the morning, everyone showed up dressed as a friendly beast. Mel wore a cheetah outfit to match Henry's, and Josh was dressed as a certain furry sidekick from a popular sci-fi film franchise. "It was the only one big enough for me," he explained, adjusting his bandolier.

What followed was a Christmas morning unlike any we had ever experienced. We always have a great time, but this year there was a lot more laughter—it's hard to keep a straight face when a giraffe tells you how much he appreciates the new gym bag you bought him. Or when you receive a hug from a panther because she loves her new dress. Or when a cheetah cub propels his

shiny new dump truck around the living room, gathering up paper and ribbons. There were more giggles and cuddles than usual too. At one point, I glanced lovingly at my husband watching his son unwrap a special set of tools, but it was tough to get too sentimental when his antlers kept flopping over one eye.

That night after everyone had left, my husband and I sat before the glowing fireplace. "Thank you," I whispered. "I know it's hard to change Christmas, but you were such a good sport."

He kissed my cheek. "Christmas isn't really about always doing everything the same, you know. It's about doing everything we can to love each other."

I snuggled up to him. "Good point," I agreed.

"Besides," he chuckled, "it's not every day I get to kiss a unicorn!"

The Christmas Dress

Kristi West Breeden

Many of my childhood Christmas memories revolve around church programs. Although Sunday mornings were dedicated to Christmas music performed by the adult choir, the children performed on a Sunday evening.

While some Christmas programs included a traditional Nativity play, most pageants were comprised of groups of children climbing on the stage to recite lines and sweetly sing "Away in a Manger" or "Silent Night." One such year, my church's kindergarten class was asked to memorize some lines for the upcoming program. Every child would have to recite a line by himself.

As a child, I was unusually shy. In fact, in many early photos I wore various degrees of a pout, as if I didn't want to be photographed, thank-you-very-much. I never enjoyed being front and center of the attention—especially in front of a camera or audience.

The teacher sent slips of paper home with each of us, and we were to rehearse our lines within the comfort of our own homes. As the program neared, the teacher was not feeling very confident about my ability to deliver this line in front of the entire church. (I'm sure we've all witnessed the various types of children on stage: the whisperer, the crier, the clothing tugger, the shouter, the nose-picker, and so on. Based on what she knew about me, the teacher was probably counting on me being the crier or the whisperer.) Picking up on this predicament, my mom decided I could use a little confidence-booster.

At home, Mom pulled out her cache of fabrics, notions, and her sewing machine and began to make a very special dress for me to wear in my Christmas program. On the evening of our program, Mom put the newly completed dress on me, fit me in Mary Janes, and styled my long hair in banana curls. When she had everything just right, the family loaded into the car and off we went to church.

With excitement building, I gathered with the rest of my class. Still not sure what would happen, the teacher lead us all to the stage where each student dutifully recited his or her line. And then it was my turn. I'm sure everyone who knew me collectively held their breath. But decked out in my finest clothes and feeling ever so grown-up, I surprised them all. Without hesitation, I stepped up to deliver my line flawlessly and clearly enough for everyone to hear. My teacher was in shock because she had never heard me speak so confidently.

My mother often recounted this story to anyone who would listen. Was it the dress that gave me the confidence to speak in front of so many people? Maybe. Did I simply have the inner fortitude to understand that I did not want to embarrass myself in front of the entire church? That's possible. Too many years have passed and I was too young to remember what was going through my mind at the time. However, it has been said that when you look good, you feel good— and a new Christmas dress is always a good idea!

SILENT NIGHT *by Susan Rios. Image © Susan Rios/Art Licensing*

A Christmas Question

Pamela Kennedy

The melody for this hauntingly beautiful Christmas carol pre-dates the lyrics by almost three centuries and was popular long before it became a Christmas carol. Tradition suggests that King Henry VIII used it to accompany romantic lyrics he wrote for Anne Boleyn and that British courtiers often danced to it. In a much less romantic setting, "Greensleeves" was sometimes played as British citizens gathered to witness public executions! Shakespeare also referred to it in his 1602 play, *The Merry Wives of Windsor*.

The author of the Christmas carol "What Child Is This?" was probably not thinking of "Greensleeves" when he composed his poem "The Manger Throne," from which the carol's lyrics were derived. William Chatterton Dix—born in Bristol, England, in 1837—was given the middle name of a poet, Thomas Chatterton, about whom his father, John Dix, had written a biography. Perhaps the surgeon and author hoped that this would help foster an interest in literature. Initially, these hopes seemed in vain, as William preferred the business world. After completing his schooling, he relocated to Glasgow, Scotland, where he started a family and became the manager of a maritime insurance company. But in his spare time, William would develop a fruitful literary career, composing poetry for use in worship.

During a particularly trying time when he was twenty-nine years old, William became seriously ill. Confined to months of bed rest, he fell into a deep depression. Despite these circumstances, it was out of this period that Dix produced a body of work from which would come more than forty hymn texts, including "As with Gladness Men of Old" as well as a Nativity poem titled "The Manger Throne."

"The Manger Throne" quickly found its way to the United States where it was published in newspapers and magazines and read aloud during Christmas church services. A few years later, an Anglican priest named Henry Ramsden Bramley and an Oxford music professor, Sir John Stainer, joined forces to edit three verses of Dix's poem and pair it with the tune of "Greensleeves." In 1871, Bramley and Stainer published their version as "What Child Is This?" in their popular work *Christmas Carols, New and Old*.

Through its winsome words and lilting melody, this lovely carol invites Christmas worshipers to meditate upon the meaning of the Nativity. And each holiday season, the carol's central question still urges individuals to ponder, "What Child Is This?"

What Child Is This?

Lyrics, William Chatterton Dix; Music, "Greensleeves" from the Old English

1. What Child is this, Who, laid to rest on Ma-ry's lap, is sleep-ing? Whom
2. Why lies He in such mean es-tate, where ox and ass are feed-ing? Good
3. So bring Him in-cense, gold and myrrh, come peas-ant, king to own Him. The

an - gels greet with an-thems sweet, while shep-herds watch are keep-ing?
Christ-ians, fear, for sin-ners here the si-lent Word is plead-ing.
King of kings sal-va-tion brings; let lov-ing hearts en-throne Him.

This, this is Christ the King, Whom shep-herds guard and an-gels sing;
Nails, spear, shall pierce Him through, the cross be borne for me, for you.
Raise, raise a song on high; the vir-gin sings her lul-la-by.

Haste, haste, to bring Him laud, the Babe, the Son of Ma - ry!
Hail, hail the Word made flesh, the Babe, the Son of Ma - ry!
Joy, joy for Christ is born, the Babe, the Son of Ma - ry!

In the Music of a Song
Grace Oldershaw

When we hear the Christmas carols,
how our hearts with gladness beat;
whether in the quiet churches
or along the busy street.
Songs of love and peace and beauty
come to us at Christmastide,
make us kinder to each other,
plant the seeds of love inside.
So we'll sing our Christmas carols
with the happy human throng,
hoping all will find a blessing
in the music of a song.

Sing a Song of Christmas
Diane McKinney

Sing a song of Christmas,
of holly and good cheer,
of church bells in the steeple
for all to see and hear

of Christmas carols ringing
in the winter air,
of tinsel-covered trees aglow
and children on the stairs.

Sing a song of Christmas,
of merriment and glee,

of stockings filled with presents,
and those beneath the tree.

Sing a song of Christmas,
of tiny tots and toys,
of eager eyes a-glowing
from all the girls and boys.

As Christmas Eve approaches,
behavior's at its best
and for all in peace on earth,
God's joys are manifest.

Sing, Sing, Sing

Keith H. Graham

Sing, weary Mary, sing.
Sing a mother's lullaby.
Kiss Jesus' tender face;
hear His welcome cry.
Sing, dazzling angels, sing.
Sing in the starry skies.
Send shepherds to the manger
wherein the Savior lies.
Sing, faithful people, sing.
Sing carols of peace and joy.
God has come to us
in a bouncing, baby boy.
Sing, sing, sing!

The Old, Old Story

Lola Neff Merritt

Let's tell that beloved old story
now that Christmastime is near;
let's lift our hearts and minds with joy
this holy time of year.
Let's read of a man and a maiden
led by angels, fulfilling God's plan;
and His Son, who was born in a stable
to bring light to the path of lost man.
Let's hear once again of poor shepherds
who sat circled around their campfires;
and listened in awe to the music
sung by God's heavenly angel choirs.

Christmas in the Heart

Betty Rosian

Let Christmas be a happy time;
let presents fill the store;
let music fill the air with chime
and joyful song galore.

But in the midst of all the glee
and celebration, find
God puts a new reality
within His people's mind.

Let hearts be humble, bowed in prayer;
let set aside be mirth,
let quiet meditation there
pay homage to Christ's birth.

A Place for Jesus

Betty Rosian

How very sad it must have been
to find no quarters in the inn.
And can you hear a maiden's sigh
that soon became a labored cry?
Could this have been what God had meant
for them, with child so imminent?
Oh, surely for a kingly birth
there had to be a place on earth
with royal purple cloth and scrim
to lay the newborn baby in.
But God, who owns the hills and dales,
has no such need of these details;
for in Christ's birth He shows us that
He dwells in every habitat.
So, Savior, I invite you come,
and make my humble heart Your home.

The Innkeeper

Edgar A. Guest

The story of an opportunity has always fascinated me. At Christmastime, I always think of the people whose privilege it was to play a part in the glory of Bethlehem. I sympathize greatly with the innkeeper there. His was a golden opportunity which he never sensed. I fancy that innkeepers then were much like innkeepers now. They have their problems and their troubles, and their inns become crowded, and guests at times must be turned away. I can imagine Joseph and Mary arriving at the crowded hostel and being told that there was no room for them. The inkeeper must have had sympathy in his breast, for he realized Mary's condition and offered her the stable. He never knew the miracle of that birth. I doubt that he ever lived to know that his inn and his stable and his act would be remembered and recalled through all the ages, so long as this world shall exist.

Someday I fancy I shall meet him in heaven. A friend may introduce him as the innkeeper at Bethlehem, and I think I know exactly what he will say to me. I have heard it said so often here on earth: "If I had known that He was a friend, I might have found room for Him." By letters of introduction, men today contrive to get accommodations which are coldly denied to total strangers. This is only human. Men always have and always will favor the well known. It is as natural that it should have happened then as that it happens now.

And so, if we ever shall meet and I shall ask that innkeeper about that first Christmas Eve at Bethlehem, I am sure he will shake his head and say, "If only I had known." Of course, he will regret it, but there never comes a Christmas Eve that I don't think of him:

"Oh, if only I had known!"
said the keeper of the inn.
"But no hint to me
    was shown,
and I didn't let them in.

"Yes, a star gleamed overhead,
but I couldn't read the skies,
and I'd given every bed
to the very rich and wise.

"And she was so poorly clad,
and he hadn't much to say!
But no room for them I had,
so I ordered them away.

"She seemed tired, and it was late
and they begged so hard, that I,
feeling sorry for her state,
in the stable let them lie.

"Had I turned some rich man out
just to make a place for them,
'twould have killed, beyond a doubt,
all my trade at Bethlehem.

"Then there came the
    Wise Men three
to the stable, with the morn,
who announced they'd come to see
the great King who had been born.

"And they brought Him
    gifts of myrrh,
costly frankincense and gold,
and a great light shone on her
in the stable, bleak and cold.

"All my patrons now are dead
and forgotten, but today
all the world to peace is led
by the ones I sent away.

"It was my unlucky fate
to be born that inn to own,
against Christ I shut my gate
oh, if only I had known!"

The Oxen
Thomas Hardy

Christmas Eve, and twelve of the clock.
"Now they are all on their knees,"
an elder said as we sat in a flock
by the embers in hearthside ease.

We pictured the meek, mild creatures where
they dwelt in their strawy pen,
nor did it occur to one of us there
to doubt they were kneeling then.

So fair a fancy few would weave
in these years! Yet, I feel,
if someone said on Christmas Eve,
"Come; see the oxen kneel,

"In the lonely barton by yonder coomb
our childhood used to know,"
I should go with him in the gloom,
hoping it might be so.

In the Middle of a Manger
Pamela Love

In the middle of a manger, the baby Jesus lay
snugly wrapped against the chill, at the break of day.
A hungry cow looked down at Him
    and said a puzzled, "Moo?"
With a baby on her breakfast hay, what was she to do?
Mary saw the startled cow, and then she slowly smiled.
She picked up her newborn Son, the long-awaited Child.
Gratefully, the cow began to nibble where He'd been;
once she'd fed, she let it be His little bed again.

Mary Shall Bring Forth a Son

Matthew 1:18–25

Now the birth of Jesus Christ was on this wise: When as his mother Mary was espoused to Joseph, before they came together, she was found with child of the Holy Ghost. Then Joseph her husband, being a just man, and not willing to make her a public example, was minded to put her away privily. But while he thought on these things, behold, the angel of the LORD appeared unto him in a dream, saying, Joseph, thou son of David, fear not to take unto thee Mary thy wife: for that which is conceived in her is of the Holy Ghost. And she shall bring forth a son, and thou shalt call his name JESUS: for he shall save his people from their sins.

Now all this was done, that it might be fulfilled which was spoken of the Lord by the prophet, saying, Behold, a virgin shall be with child, and shall bring forth a son, and they shall call his name Emmanuel, which being interpreted is, God with us. Then Joseph being raised from sleep did as the angel of the Lord had bidden him, and took unto him his wife: And knew her not till she had brought forth her firstborn son: and he called his name Jesus.

The Shepherds Finding the Infant Christ *by William Brassey Hole.*
Image © Look and Learn/Bridgeman Images

And This Shall Be a Sign Unto You
Luke 2:8–20

And there were in the same country shepherds abiding in the field, keeping watch over their flock by night. And, lo, the angel of the Lord came upon them, and the glory of the Lord shone round about them: and they were sore afraid. And the angel said unto them, Fear not: for, behold, I bring you good tidings of great joy, which shall be to all people. For unto you is born this day in the city of David a Saviour, which is Christ the Lord. And this shall be a sign unto you; Ye shall find the babe wrapped in swaddling clothes, lying in a manger.

And suddenly there was with the angel a multitude of the heavenly host praising God, and saying, Glory to God in the highest, and on earth peace, good will toward men.

And it came to pass, as the angels were gone away from them into heaven, the shepherds said one to another, Let us now go even unto Bethlehem, and see this thing which is come to pass, which the Lord hath made known unto us. And they came with haste, and found Mary, and Joseph, and the babe lying in a manger. And when they had seen it, they made known abroad the saying which was told them concerning this child. And all they that heard it wondered at those things which were told them by the shepherds.

But Mary kept all these things, and pondered them in her heart. And the shepherds returned, glorifying and praising God for all the things that they had heard and seen, as it was told unto them.

An Angel Announcing to the Shepherds *by William Brassey Hole.*
Image © Look and Learn/Bridgeman Images

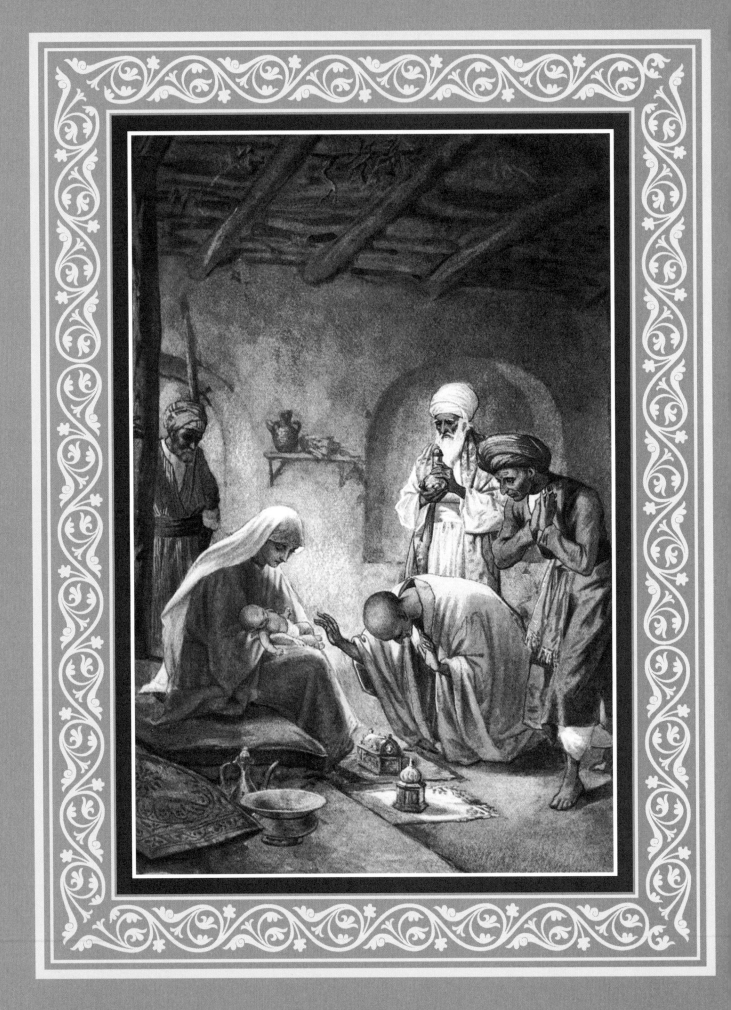

They Presented Unto Him Gifts

Matthew 2:1–12

Now when Jesus was born in Bethlehem of Judaea in the days of Herod the king, behold, there came wise men from the east to Jerusalem, Saying, Where is he that is born King of the Jews? for we have seen his star in the east, and are come to worship him.

When Herod the king had heard these things, he was troubled, and all Jerusalem with him. And when he had gathered all the chief priests and scribes of the people together, he demanded of them where Christ should be born.

And they said unto him, In Bethlehem of Judaea: for thus it is written by the prophet, And thou Bethlehem, in the land of Juda, art not the least among the princes of Juda: for out of thee shall come a Governor, that shall rule my people Israel.

Then Herod, when he had privily called the wise men, enquired of them diligently what time the star appeared. And he sent them to Bethlehem, and said, Go and search diligently for the young child; and when ye have found him, bring me word again, that I may come and worship him also.

When they had heard the king, they departed; and, lo, the star, which they saw in the east, went before them, till it came and stood over where the young child was. When they saw the star, they rejoiced with exceeding great joy. And when they were come into the house, they saw the young child with Mary his mother, and fell down, and worshipped him: and when they had opened their treasures, they presented unto him gifts; gold, and frankincense and myrrh. And being warned of God in a dream that they should not return to Herod, they departed into their own country another way.

THREE KINGS WORSHIPING CHRIST *by William Brassey Hole.*
Image © Look and Learn/Bridgeman Images

The Spirit of Giving

Kate Douglas Wiggin

When the Child of Nazareth was born, the sun, according to a Bosnian legend, "leaped in the heavens, and the stars around it danced. A peace came over mountain and forest. Even the rotten stump stood straight and healthy on the green hillside. The grass was beflowered with open blossoms, incense sweet as myrrh pervaded upland and forest, birds sang on the mountaintop, and all gave thanks to the great God."

It is naught but an old folktale, but it has truth hidden at its heart; for a strange, subtle force, a spirit of genial goodwill, a newborn kindness seem to animate child and man alike when the world pays its tribute to the "heaven-sent youngling," as the poet Drummond calls the infant Christ.

When the Wise Men rode from the east into the west on that "first, best Christmas night," they bore on their saddlebows three caskets filled with gold and frankincense and myrrh to be laid at the feet of the manger-cradled babe of Bethlehem. Beginning with this old, old journey, the spirit of giving crept into the world's heart. As the Magi came bearing gifts, so do we also; gifts that relieve wants, gifts that are sweet and fragrant with friendship, gifts that breathe love, gifts that mean service, gifts inspired still by the star that shone over the city of David more than two thousand years ago.

Then hang the green coronet of the Christmas tree with glittering baubles and jewels of flame; heap offerings on its emerald branches; bring the Yule log to the firing; deck the house with holly and mistletoe,

And all the bells
on earth shall ring
On Christmas Day
in the morning.

Bethlehem of Judea
Author Unknown

A little child,
a shining star.
A stable rude,
the door ajar.
Yet in that place,
so crude, forlorn,
the Hope of all
the world was born.

A Christmas Hymn
Christina G. Rossetti

Love came down at Christmas,
love all lovely, love divine;
love was born at Christmas—
star and angels gave the sign.

Love shall be our token;
love be yours and love be mine,
love to God and all men,
love for plea and gift and sign.

FOLLOWING THE LIGHT *by Abraham Hunter.*
Image © Abraham Hunter/MHS Licensing

Starlight on a Stable
Pamela Love

Starlight on a stable,
starlight in a stall
warmed the Lord of Ages
as a Baby small.
Starlight on the manger
helped the shepherds see
the Baby whom the
    angels sang
at His Nativity.

The Twelve Days of Christmas

Rebecca Barlow Jordan

They opened their treasures and presented him with gifts. —MATTHEW 2:11 (NIV)

When I was a child, my family didn't practice older, liturgical traditions, so I had always thought the "Twelve Days of Christmas" began twelve days before Christmas and ended with our gift exchange and celebration on Christmas Day. One year, I even presented my husband with a special gift each of the twelve days leading up to Christmas.

We taught our children to prepare for Christmas, often by using a felt, homemade Advent calendar. We tucked special things to do into each day's pocket: encourage a friend, take cookies to homebound neighbors, read a Christmas Bible passage, or do something nice for someone. We wanted to help shift the emphasis from receiving to giving. But, like everyone else, after we opened our gifts on Christmas morning, we tossed the wrappings and packed away the trappings of Christmas until the following year.

On a study trip to Israel one year, I walked where Jesus once walked and viewed the place where the Christ-Child could have been born, as well as a possible site of the Magi's visit. As a result of that trip, I experienced my own "epiphany." I returned determined to celebrate this divine season in a deeper way than I previously had.

As my research led me to the history and meaning of the Twelve Days of Christmas, I discovered that the season is celebrated in various ways. I thought how special it would be to truly begin our celebrations on the actual day of Christmas and continue for twelve more. And as I looked at the Epiphany—or the twelfth day—I realized how we could learn so much from those wise Magi who visited the long-awaited Jesus.

The Wise Men had spent years in preparation for the coming King, as they studied the stars so carefully designed by their Creator. And when their investigation revealed perfect alignment in the heavens for the divinely staged event, they prepared for and began their long journey. But they didn't set out empty-handed. They carried extravagant gifts worthy of a King: gold, frankincense, and myrrh. The Wise Men traveled far in search of the Star and its long-prophesied revelation: a king would soon be born. But not just any king. This King had the stamp of heaven and the name of Jesus, our Savior.

As I thought about the Wise Men—and even of God's own long preparation for the coming King, His own Son, through centuries of waiting—I wondered: how could we prepare our hearts more with reverent remembrance for this season? And how could we celebrate in an even greater way this miraculous event? No matter how much or how little we have, we can find a way to celebrate Christmas every day of the year: through intentional acts of kindness or generous words of encouragement, with forgiveness offered freely, and love given unselfishly. Whatever we give or do, if it's offered in the name of Jesus, our gifts can be extravagant sacrifices worthy of a King.

There's More to Christmas
Author Unknown

There's more, much more, to Christmas
than candlelight and cheer;
it's the spirit of sweet friendship
that brightens all the year;
it's thoughtfulness and kindness;
it's hope reborn again,
for peace, for understanding,
and for goodwill to men!

Christmastide
Susan Sundwall

Christmastide rolls from shore to shore,
calling us to the stable once more.
Hungry hearts cradle the tiny King;
souls rise up to worship and sing.
Holly and ivy, forest and tree
come to Him on bended knee.
Creation quiets to welcome the morn,
for love and life have now been born.

Christmas Joy
Virginia Blanck Moore

Half the fun of Christmas
is the deep-down pleasure
we get from giving others
joy in fullest measure.

Half the fun of Christmas
is shopping thoughtfully
for gifts that bring
    a glow to those
who find them 'neath
      their tree.

Half the fun of Christmas
is baking things to share,
and sending messages of love
to those for whom we care.

Half the fun of Christmas
is walking down the street
just wishing health
    and happiness
to those we chance to meet.

Half the fun? Nay, all the fun
is the heartfelt pleasure
we get from giving other folks
joy in fullest measure.

Image © Yuganov Konstantin/Shutterstock

The Simple Joys of Christmas

Rebecca Barlow Jordan

The simple joys of Christmas:
loved ones, family, friends;
exchanging love and happiness
to make a perfect blend
of holidays and memories
to cherish all year long;
while bright and cheerful carolers
add their Christmas song.
And in the silent celebration,
like the shepherds of old,
our hearts rejoice again in the
sweetest story ever told.

ISBN-13: 978-0-8249-1352-6

Published by Ideals
An imprint of Worthy Publishing Group
A division of Worthy Media, Inc.
Nashville, Tennessee

Printed and bound in the U.S.A.
Printed on Weyerhauser Lynx. The paper used in this publication meets the minimum requirements of American National Standard for Information Sciences—Permanence of Paper for Printed Materials, ANSI Z39.48-1984.

Publisher, Peggy Schaefer
Editor, Melinda L. R. Rumbaugh
Designer, Marisa Jackson
Permissions and Research, Kristi Breeden
Copy Editors, Kaye Dacus, Hannah Lamb

Cover: *Snow Village I* by Jim Mitchell. Image © Jim Mitchell/Advocate Art
Inside front cover: *Snowy Peace* by Lisa Graa Jensen. Image © Lisa Graa Jensen/Bridgeman Images
Inside back cover: *Snow Geese* by Lisa Graa Jensen. Image © Lisa Graa Jensen/Bridgeman Images

Additional art credits: art for "Bits & Pieces," "Family Recipes," back cover spot art, and spot art for pages 1 and 36 by Kathryn Rusynyk.
"What Child Is This?" sheet music by Dick Torrans, Melode, Inc.

ACKNOWLEDGMENTS

LUNA, ANDREW L. "Sparse Decorations" from *Unwrap the Memories* © Andrew Luna. All rights reserved. Used by permission. OUR THANKS to the following authors or their heirs: Georgia B. Adams, Anne Kennedy Brady, Kristi West Breeden, Lansing Christman, Lucille Crumley, Edgar A. Guest, Keith H. Graham, Pauline Havard, Elma Helgason, Kay Hoffman, Linda Heuring, Rebecca Barlow Jordan, Pamela Kennedy, Lucille King, Pamela Love, Nadine Brothers Lybarger, Alice Arlene MacCulloch, Diane McKinney, Lola Neff Merritt, Virginia Blanck Moore, A. Earl Morris, Grace Oldershaw, Betty Rosian, Judy Schwab, Eileen Spinelli, Susan Sundwall, and Ellie Van Wicklen.
    Scripture quotations, unless otherwise indicated, are taken from King James Version (KJV). Scripture quotation marked NIV is taken from The Holy Bible, New International Version®, NIV® Copyright ©1973, 1978, 1984, 2011 by Biblica, Inc.®

Used by permission. All rights reserved worldwide.
    Every effort has been made to establish ownership and use of each selection in this book. If contacted, the publisher will be pleased to rectify any inadvertent errors or omissions in subsequent editions.

Join the community of *Ideals* readers on Facebook at:
www.facebook.com/IdealsMagazine
Readers are invited to submit original poetry and prose for possible use in future publications. Please send no more than four typed submissions to: *Ideals* submissions, Worthy Publishing Group, 6100 Tower Circle, Suite 210, Franklin, Tennessee 37067. Manuscripts will be returned if a self-addressed stamped envelope is included.